Jolie's Garden

Jolie's Garden

Patricia Anne Tomkinson

ATHENA PRESS
LONDON

Jolie's Garden
Copyright © Patricia Anne Tomkinson 2007

ISBN 10-digit: 1 84748 090 X
ISBN 13-digit: 978 1 84748 090 3

First Published 2007 by
ATHENA PRESS
Queen's House, 2 Holly Road
Twickenham TW1 4EG
United Kingdom

Printed for Athena Press

This book is dedicated with love and gratitude
to Julie Brett-Bellis, spiritual teacher and light worker
(www.lightsourcejulie.moonfruit.com),
who inspired me to write *Jolie's Garden*.

Contents

Jolie's Garden

Jolie's house had a garden,
Filled with beautiful flowers.
While Mummy did the housework,
She'd play outside for hours.

She loved her swing and trampoline
And little Wendyhouse
And all the games that she played
With her dog, cat and mouse.

Best of all she loved the games
That no one knew about.
When the grown-ups were inside
Her little friends came out.

Little People came to her
And shared in all her games:
The fairies, elves and pixies,
The leprechauns and gnomes.

The garden was full of them
They all lived there, you see.
Their homes were hidden deep inside
Each flower, plant and tree.

Only Jolie had seen them,
And one thing she did know –
That it was their job indeed
To make her garden grow.

They took care of her flowers,
Brought out trees in blossom;
And when Daddy mowed, they tried
To keep the daisies' heads on.

Daddy worked so hard outside
He lay down on the floor,
But Jolie knew that her friends
Did all the hard work before.

Shola

Shola was a fairy,
The prettiest ever seen.
Her wings were gold and silver,
Speckled with glittering green.

Her long wavy hair was tied
With ribbon sparkly and bright.
Her clothes were spun from gold threads:
Beautiful, shimmering light.

She lived in Jolie's garden
Inside a giant, red rose,
Its perfume did surround her
From her head down to her toes.

Shola was so very shy
And was too afraid to speak.
If she was brave enough to try
It just came out as a squeak!

She longed to play with Jolie
Like her other fairy friends.
And this could easily have been
Where Shola's sad story ends.

Jolie had never seen her,
For she always hid away,
But things changed for the better
On one particular day.

Shola's curiosity
Encouraged her then to peep
At Jolie in the garden
On her deckchair fast asleep.

So Shola sat beside her,
Then flew upon her shoulder.
They could be best of friends
If she was a bit bolder.

Then Jolie stirred from her sleep
And then opened wide her eyes.
Seeing Shola beside her
Made her startle with surprise.

Shola quickly spread her wings,
Intent on flying away,
But Jolie called out softly,
'Please stay here awhile and play.'

The two became acquainted,
And that day became the start
Of a new relationship:
Friends impossible to part!

Shanice

Shanice was the oldest fairy,
So beautiful and wise.
She came down to Jolie's garden
From bluest of blue skies.

A rainbow bridge transported her
From heaven down to earth.
She had so much work to do here –
Would try for all her worth.

It was her task from this day on
To help each flower and tree,
Every plant, bush and blade of grass
As far as the eye could see.

She told all the Nature Spirits,
Fairies, gnomes and elves,
To set about in growing things
And tend to each themselves.

She also let them laugh and play
And most of all to sing.
Shanice did know that music sweet
Such merriment would bring.

She said the most important thing
Was to try with all their might
To spread amongst all living things
A beautiful white light.

'The light is now there within you,'
Shanice did say with glee.
'To shine the light is so easy
You must just follow me.'

They watched then in awe as Shanice
Silently shut her eyes;
She opened up her pale pink wings
And then began to rise.

Then she opened her mouth and blew
Upon the flowers with care.
A beautiful white light came down
Filling up all the air.

It shimmered upon the flowers,
Sparkling with flecks of gold.
The flowers shone with energy,
Wonderful to behold.

The roses seemed more colourful
Than they ever had before;
Their petals were all so lovely;
Their scent you would adore.

The white light had done its work here
And blessed each flower with health:
Now all of Nature's Spirits must
Go do the same with stealth.

'Just discover the light within
For you know it is there,'
Shanice told all of her workers.
'It's simple, to be fair.

'If you trust that you can do it,
The white light then will rise;
Then blow it out all around you –
Success will be your prize.

'The trees and plants and the flowers
Will grow beautiful and strong.
The white light will then protect them,
They'll look lovely all day long!'

Two Little Leprechauns

When Jolie first saw Shanice,
It was by the old cherry tree.
She thought she was so beautiful
And just as pretty as could be.

'I'm four years old,' said Jolie.
'And how old, may I ask, are you?'
'A bit older than you, Jolie –
One hundred and seventy-two.'

'How can you be?' asked Jolie
'I just can't believe it, never!'
Shanice replied, 'Well don't you know?
We fairies do live for ever.'

'You've got a nice green dress on,'
Said Jolie, as they sat by the pond.
'Your hair's the same colour as mine,
It's a sort of yellowy-blonde.'

Then they heard a squelching noise,
By the edge of the pond in the mud.
And there, staring right back at them,
Two tiny wee leprechauns stood.

'We've come from Ireland,' said one,
'Across choppy oceans and seas.
We'd very much like to live here,
If that is all right with you, please?'

'You are welcome,' Jolie said,
'As long as you promise and say
That you will help in the garden;
Yes, then you may certainly stay.'

'We're called Ashling and Felan,
Now please will you give us some tea?
We've had such a tiring journey,
And we're as hungry as can be.'

Ashling was a sweet small thing –
An impish twinkle in her eyes.
Felan looked very mischievous
(Really wanting to make mud pies!)

'May we live under the rhubarb bush?'
Said Ashling with a childlike stare.
But Jolie had a strange feeling
They might be a rascally pair.

'We will be good and work hard –
We promise to right from the start!'
Then Jolie knew that they were both
Really very good in their hearts.

Just then Ashling's foot got stuck
In the mud – oh, what a fluster!
So Felan pulled upon her leg
With all the strength he could muster!

Jolie and Shanice then helped
And at last it came out… stinking!
They were all splattered with the mud,
But they just fell about laughing!

Jolie squealed, 'You will get us
Into all such mischief, you will see.
But I'm also pretty sure
That the best of friends we will be!'

Jelly Dessert

Jolie wanted some jelly,
It was her favourite dessert.
She went into the kitchen
And then tugged at Mummy's skirt.

'Please can you make some jelly?
I would like it for my tea.
I'll take it in the garden,
I won't make a mess, you'll see.'

The jelly was so tasty,
Guess who enjoyed it the most?
It was Ashling and Felan,
They spread it onto some toast!

Then they thought it would be fun
To spread it onto their feet;
This was surely much better
Than having it to eat!

Daddy was in the sun lounge,
Reading his paper after tea.
He heard mention of jelly,
And thought, *Is there some for me?*

He left his paper and went out
To find his little daughter.
He wanted to ask what flavour
Jelly Mummy might have bought her!

Ashling and Felan ran amok,
Their jelly-feet made them slide.
They thought it best to run away
When they saw Daddy come outside.

They ran into the sun lounge,
Treading sticky blobs of jelly,
Then jumped on Daddy's newspaper
And even on the telly!

Now Jolie would be in trouble
For being an untidy girl.
She'd had such fun with the jelly,
She'd been in such a whirl!

Her toys were scattered on the lawn,
With some in a great big mound.
When Daddy looked for Jolie,
She was nowhere to be found!

She'd gone to play at hide-and-seek
And was behind the garden shed.
Daddy was getting very cross,
It was nearly time for her bed.

At last he found her and took her
Back to view the mess he'd found.
'Jolie, you must learn from this
Not to leave your toys on the ground!'

Daddy went back to the sun lounge
And couldn't believe what he saw:
For there was jelly everywhere…
More and more and more!

'Now, who's done this?' cried Daddy,
Feeling suddenly in a daze,
'It's even on my newspaper…
It's smeared across every page!'

'Oh Daddy, you must learn from this,'
Jolie wisely did implore.
'Next time pick up your newspaper…
Don't leave it on the floor!'

Jolie's Poorly Day

Poor Jolie had a cold one day
And had to stay in bed.
Mummy brought her some bread and jam
To make sure she was fed.

'Now you must stay in bed,' said Mum,
'So that you will get well.
If you get up and run about
Be sure that I can tell!'

Mum disappeared downstairs again,
Giving Jolie a kiss.
All my little friends, thought Jolie,
Today they will be missed.

They missed her too, the leprechauns,
The fairies and the elves;
So they decided they would go
And find her by themselves.

They climbed up the wobbly drainpipe
One by one, up they sped –
Not just one or two of them came,
But more than one hundred!

They tapped upon the windowpane
So that Jolie would hear.
She looked up from her bed and thought,
Oh dear, oh dear, oh dear!

Jolie opened up the window
Asking for a quiet tread.
They jumped inside and clambered up
On top of Jolie's bed.

'You must just whisper,' Jolie said,
'Or Mummy will hear us.
I don't want your mischief today
To be coming near us!'

'Ooh, strawberry jam!' yelled out Ashling.
'I'll put it on my feet.'
'Oh no you don't!' scolded Jolie,
'You'll get it on my sheet!'

'I'll put it on my hands instead,
And then I think I'll try
To swing up onto the lampshade,'
Came Ashling's swift reply.

And before Jolie could stop her,
She jumped onto the light.
Then she swung on it round and round
Spinning with all her might.

Her sticky, jammy fingers left
Red marks on the ceiling,
Then she lost her grip – and to earth
She was quickly reeling.

She landed back on Jolie's bed,
Wow, what a super trick!
But Ashling, feeling dizzy, wailed,
'I think I will to be sick!'

Just then they heard Jolie's Mummy
Running up the stairs.
They scampered quickly off the bed
And hid behind the chairs.

Mummy looked up at the ceiling,
Plastered in strawberry jam.
Jolie just calmly lay in bed,
Innocent as a lamb!

'On no!' said Mummy, quite perplexed.
'How did you manage that?'
'I flicked my spoon,' fibbed Jolie,
'And the jam just went SPLAT!'

'Do try and be good,' Mummy begged.
'Your ceiling is a sight!'
Then she went up to the window
And shut it nice and tight.

Mummy then went downstairs again,
The guests knew they should go,
But Mummy had closed their escape –
She'd locked the only window!

'You'll have to sneak out down the stairs
When Mummy's back is turned,'
Said Jolie, peeping through the door…
Oh how her tummy churned!

The guests bolted out of the door
But they stopped at the stairs.
Jolie whispered 'No, not like that!
You'll have to go down in pairs!'

So, two by two, then down they crept,
Walking close in file.
Then when they'd sneaked past Mum,
They all just ran a mile!

Swimming with Dolphins

Daddy woke Jolie one morning
And she soon shouted out 'Hooray!'
For Daddy had good news to tell –
They were going on holiday!

'We're off to Florida,' he said,
'Where there's dolphins, theme parks and rides.
There will be shops for Mummy
And lots more to do there, besides.'

Florida was just beautiful;
Sparkling sea and golden sand.
Daddy arranged what they would do,
All kinds of fun things had been planned.

Mummy loved all of the shops there –
So many bags, shoes and dresses,
The coats and hats and jewellery,
Just masses upon masses!

Now when in the biggest toy shop,
Jolie had just happened to spy
The most gorgeous doll ever seen –
She thought, *My, oh my, oh my!*

'Daddy, please buy that doll!' she shrieked
At him as loudly as she could.
'You ought to treat me on holiday,
You should, you should, you really should!'

'But Jolie, we have just got here,
There's so much to do and to see.
We came here to do other things,
Not to go on a spending spree!'

Then Jolie did lose her temper,
She screamed loudly and stamped her feet.
'If you don't buy the doll for me
I'll yell all up and down the street!'

Daddy was not impressed by this
And he took her outside the shop.
'No swimming with dolphins,' he said,
'If your tantrum doesn't soon stop!'

Jolie calmed down and was sorry –
The dolphins just couldn't be missed –
Swimming with them was at the top
Of her 'Best Things To Do' wish list.

The highlight of the holiday
Was without doubt going to be
Swimming along with the dolphins
In the beautiful, azure sea.

Jolie was very excited
As they waited upon the sand,
Then they all ran to the water,
Laughing together, hand in hand.

The dolphins kept them spellbound,
Swimming round and round them for hours.
Dolphins can make anyone smile –
Jolie thought they had magic powers!

Diving, jumping up and splashing,
And making their wonderful sounds,
Spreading their joy and endless fun,
Causing pleasure that knew no bounds.

Jolie was so full of joy,
As were Mummy and Daddy, too;
But now their fun day had ended,
And they had to leave, this they knew.

They said goodbye to the dolphins –
Daddy had a tear in his eye.
They vowed to come again one day –
Maybe next year they would try.

Jolie went to sleep and did dream
Of the graceful dolphins that night.
She seemed to drift up slowly
Into a wonderful bright light.

She was swimming in a sparkling
And shimmering deep blue sea,
And then she could see the dolphins –
She saw them plainly as could be.

They swam towards her so swiftly,
Moving with such great ease and grace.
Soon they came up close beside her,
She could see each gentle face.

The dolphins seemed to talk to her
And she thought that she heard them say,
'Jolie, promise to be carefree
And to enjoy each lovely day.

'Enjoy the sun and warm blue sea,
And all nature that surrounds you:
The mountains, the trees, the flowers,
And listen to natures' sounds too.

'These are the things of great beauty
That will give you far more pleasure
Than any doll or man-made toy
That you think that you might treasure.'

The dolphins were just satisfied
Each sunny day to enjoy…
The bliss of the sun's warm rays
Was much better than any toy!

Next morning when Jolie awoke,
To Daddy she did then hurry.
'I had a magic dream last night!'
She blurted out in a flurry.

'Daddy, sorry I made a fuss,
Shouting about that doll for hours.
There are things far more important –
Like dolphins, mountains and flowers!'

Daddy was much impressed by this,
He thought her words very wise.
Later that day he bought the doll
As a well-deserved surprise!

The Moonlight Fairy

There was a knock on the window,
When Jolie had just gone to bed,
A lovely fairy hovered there,
'May I come in?' she gently said.

'Open the window just a crack
And do let me enter inside.
A single shaft of pure moonlight
Is all I need on which to glide.

'Shimmering down on the moonbeams,
I will alight upon your world –
Dressed up in my finest attire,
My hair so beautifully curled.

'How do you like my gold-spun dress?
It's so pretty, don't you agree?
The Sunlight Fairies did make it
Especially and just for me.

'It is spun from finest sunbeams,
Adorned with a sprinkling of stars.
I wear it to go to parties
On Venus, Jupiter and Mars.

'If you like, I'll ask the fairies
To perhaps make a dress for you.
Little earth girls just like yourself
Deserve to dress prettily, too.

'I'll bring it when you are sleeping
And you can wear it in your dreams;
We'll eat fairy cakes and chocolate
Till our dresses burst at the seams!'

The Fairy Dance

Lightfoot was such a sprightly fellow,
A handsome elf was he.
He lived at the end of the garden,
Under the roots of the sycamore tree.

He liked to keep himself to himself,
Was always serious.
But if the fairies and elves did play,
He suddenly became quite curious.

However, he never joined their games,
Just kept right on working.
He kept so busy tending the trees,
He worked all day long, never shirking!

Climbing daily up the tall, tall trees –
No problem, that, for him!
He travelled along from branch to branch
Swinging easily from limb to limb.

The leaves he devotedly tended,
Made them healthy and strong.
But when the first leaves fell in autumn
He was upset nearly all day long.

He loved the colours, the beautiful greens,
All sorts of lovely shades;
And even more so in the autumn
When they floated down in golden cascades.

On one particular autumn day
The fairies did decide
That they would hold their most special dance
And perform it at night with great pride.

Every autumn when it was full moon
They had a ballerina dance.
They would practise hard for weeks before
Each step they would try hard to enhance.

Every fairy moved with style and grace –
Elegant and flowing.
They wanted their audience to enjoy
A show that would leave their hearts glowing.

But alas there was one small problem –
No dresses had they to wear!
The fairy who made their special clothes
Had gone away, it seemed so unfair!

Lightfoot happened to hear their distress
Then he had an idea!
He said, 'I think I can help you.
I can make you some lovely new gear!'

They were very surprised to hear this –
Slightly sceptical too –
Lightfoot stayed in the trees all day long,
What sewing could he know how to do?

A fairy whispered, 'How can it be?
It's a joke! He can't sew;
Perhaps he has the idea,' she giggled,
'That clothes, by themselves, just simply grow!'

'My leaves are beautiful,' said the elf,
'At this time of the year.
Their colours are such rich reds and golds –
Ideal for your dance, it would appear.'

It would be lovely indeed to dress
In leaves from head to toe,
But how would the leaves stick together?
They had no one who knew how to sew.

'I know!' said one. 'Perhaps we could ask
Dear Jolie what to do.
She is so very clever and kind,
She'll have lots of ideas I'm sure, too.'

Jolie was on the small garden swing
When up the lawn they came –
A swarm of tiny fairies, anxious,
And excitedly calling her name.

'Jolie, please, you must help us!' they begged,
Talking in a babble.
'Calm down!' she shouted out above them,
'You sound just like a rioting rabble!'

'We need new clothes for our fairy dance –
Lightfoot suggested leaves –
But how do we make them wearable?
How do we do things like put in sleeves?

'We have no fairy who can sew them,
We haven't got a clue.'
'I know!' said Jolie, smiling brightly,
'We can stick them together with glue.'

Later that day came the tricky bit,
Sticking leaves with care,
Till all the little fairy dresses
Had been finished with much skill and flair.

The dresses looked very beautiful,
In brown and gold and red.
'A job worth doing,' beamed Jolie.
'They are so gorgeous,' she proudly said.

The fairies were so truly grateful,
To Jolie they did say,
'You must come and watch our fairy dance,
It will be a magical display!

'Come down to the wood beside the lake,
At the stroke of midnight.'
'I can't come out that late!' gasped Jolie.
'Mummy would have a terrible fright!'

'Of course, how silly we are!' they said.
'That simply would not do.
Well if you really can't come to us,
Then we will happily come to you!

'We'll put on a show in your garden,
Down beside the fish pond.
Then all your frogs can watch us as well,
Of them we are exceedingly fond.'

Little Jolie went to bed that night,
But didn't go to sleep.
She kept creeping up to the window
And opening the curtains to peep.

Exactly at the stroke of midnight,
The fairies did appear.
In a circle they stood on the lawn…
Jolie just wanted to shout and cheer!

Each fairy carried a little bell;
When the dance did begin
The bells started to tinkle and chime,
Sending the fairies into a spin.

So they twirled and they pirouetted,
Leaping high in the air.
The frogs did climb up out of the pond
They couldn't do much else except stare!

They thought it was truly amazing
Then they all leapt about.
It was the frogs' way of dancing
Of that there could not be any doubt!

The elves had a very special job,
Which they could do with ease.
They sprinkled the golden fairy dust
From the branches of the tallest of the trees.

Yes, from the very highest branches
The fairy dust did fall.
The dark air just glittered and sparkled
With a thousand gold speckles in all.

The black velvet sky was softly lit
By the silvery moon.
Jolie stood at her window entranced –
It looked just like a huge white balloon!

Ashling and Felan helped too, of course,
Joyfully they did sing.
They climbed up on the garden wind chimes
And were merrily making them ring!

Lightfoot knew that he couldn't resist –
He had to dance as well.
He'd never had so much fun in his life
As the other fairies all could tell.

The Little People were astounded
That Lightfoot had such flair
He then picked up each of the fairies,
Twirling them, one by one, in the air!

So they danced until they were dizzy
Till they could dance no more.
Then they all flopped down onto the grass,
It was much better than they'd wished for.

The fairies looked up at the window
Giving Jolie a wave.
She applauded her friends quite wildly,
For the lovely performance they gave.

But next morning Jolie was tired,
Yawning behind her hand.
Mummy and Daddy didn't notice…
There was something they couldn't understand.

Daddy said, 'There was no wind last night,
But I'm sure I could hear
The clinking of our garden wind chimes
After midnight, ringing loud and clear.'

'Yes, I heard them too,' Mummy answered.
I thought, how could it be?
I nearly got right out of my bed
To look out of the window and see.'

I'm so glad she didn't, thought Jolie,
That would have stopped the fun.
The fairies would have hidden away;
The poor frogs would have had to run!

Jolie didn't see her friends that day –
They were inside their flowers.
Everyone was simply exhausted…
They just lay asleep for hours and hours!

My Unicorn

Lightfoot had a warm cosy home
Under the roots of his tree.
Jolie was trying to find him
'I wonder just where can he be?'

She knelt by his sycamore tree.
'Are you in there?' she loudly cried.
'It's really past my bedtime now,'
Lightfoot's sleepy voice then replied.

'Please do not disturb my slumber,
Lest my unicorn deigns to call.
He visits in the twilight hours,
When the soft veil of dusk does fall.

'I see him wrapped in smoky cloud,
Descending slowly from the sky.
The stars weave their dance about him,
Angels bless him when passing by.

'With fingers entwined in his mane,
Upon his silky back I ride,
To wondrous realms not of this world,
Where magical creatures abide.

'From my unicorn's silver horn
Falls a fountain of rainbow light,
Showering me with wisdom and love
As we travel on through the night.

'In the clear white searching light of morning
I wonder, *Was it all a dream?*
Yet, encircling my tree trunk,
I see a glinting rainbow stream.

'A million dazzling sparkles
Of unicorn light meets my eyes,
And I know I will meet again
With my unicorn from the skies.'

Nice Thoughts

Jolie went outside one day
And sat on the wooden seat.
The Little People heard her –
She did loudly stamp her feet!

A frown they could see clearly
Upon her little red face.
She wasn't like their Jolie,
Of her there was not a trace!

'What is the matter, Jolie?'
Asked Shola. 'You're in a mood?'
'I am!' said Jolie crossly.
'Mummy says that I've been rude!

'I don't like Mummy today,'
Sulked Jolie. 'She is so mean.
'I think I'll roll in some mud
And not keep my new clothes clean!'

'Thoughts are all real,' said Shola,
'A bit like a boomerang.
Your thoughts, they will come back
And over you they will hang.

'Think good thoughts and you will find
That nice things will soon occur.
If your thoughts are miserable,
You'll cause a terrible stir.

'A black cloud hangs over you,
Right now, just as we do speak.
It will make you unhappy,
Your life will seem dull and bleak.

'But if you can change your thoughts,
From grumpy ones into kind,
The black cloud will disappear
And happiness you'll find.'

'All right,' said Jolie, 'I'll try,
But Mummy is in a mood.
I did make her very cross;
I refused to eat my food!'

Jolie went back in the house
And gave Mummy lots of smiles.
'My Mummy is wonderful,
She's the best Mum by miles.

'I think I'll be good today
And do some jobs to help her.
I'll even tidy my toys;
We can make tea together.'

Mummy was so pleased to see
Jolie was happy again –
'Let's go to the park,' she said.
'Your bad mood has gone, it's plain.'

Mummy and Jolie did laugh,
It was much better to be
Happy, smiling, having fun,
Than sulking in misery.

The fairies smiled knowingly,
For they could so clearly see
All the bright, golden sunbeams
Shining on Mummy and Jolie.

Poppies

There is a place, Jolie knows not where,
But in her dreams she is taken there –
To a sea of poppies, ruby-red,
And a pure blue sky above her head.

Rippling winds make the poppies shiver,
Tiny fairies do make them quiver
As through their stems they do run and shriek,
Darting, jumping, playing hide-and-seek.

Their laughter sprinkles right through the field,
Till, worn out, to exhaustion they yield.
Poppies fall still, no murmur is heard,
But the fairies are soon to be stirred.

A playful cloud skips across the sky
And the elves spring up, to leap on high.
Landing so deftly upon the cloud,
They chuckle and sing and laugh out loud.

With wings aflutter, fairies land there,
And, all aboard, they float through the air.
In the next field they jump down once more,
Into a sea of tulips galore.

Hide-and-seek absorbs them yet again,
Till the sun sets, replaced by the rain.
The game ends until another day,
When the friends will then resume their play.

The Rainbow

Right at the end of the garden
Was a patch that Daddy did ignore;
It really was most untidy,
With dandelions and weeds galore.

But there was a splendid toadstool,
Hidden away from general view.
It was the proud home of a gnome
Who went by the name of Jim Jew.

Jim Jew lived down amongst the weeds,
He was glad it was overgrown,
It meant Daddy never came near
And his toadstool was left alone.

He polished the shiny red top,
Taking care with its large white spots,
Then he'd sit upon it for hours,
Admiring it lots and lots!

One day when it was raining hard,
Jolie appeared out of the house.
She wore her rain coat and wellies
And was holding her small pet mouse.

Jim Jew ran up to greet Jolie
And her little mouse, Smokey Ash –
He often rode on his back;
He could run as fast as a flash.

'We're going to the pond,' said Jolie,
'To meet with Ashling and Felan.
What a shame it's raining!' she cried,
Then away she quickly ran.

Ashling and Felan were waiting,
But didn't notice her coming.
They seemed rather preoccupied,
As though both looking for something.

They gazed up at the dull grey sky,
Turning their heads from side to side.
'What is the matter?' asked Jolie.
'Oh look!' Ashling suddenly cried.

The sun came out between the clouds,
Spreading bright, golden shafts of light.
'Rain and sun together!' she yelled.
'We could see a rainbow... we might!'

Jolie, Jim Jew and Smokey Ash
All raised up their eyes to the sky,
And suddenly there before them
Was a rainbow, arching up high.

'It is beautiful!' sighed Jolie.
'Tell me, is it true or pretend?
Is there a pot of gold, as claimed,
At the rainbow's very end?'

'Why yes, it's true!' Felan replied.
'It's there for anyone to find;
But just what sort of gold it is
Depends wholly on your own mind.'

'What do you mean?' queried Jolie,
For she didn't quite understand.
'The gold is what your heart desires…
Your own wish, be it small or grand.'

'I see,' she said. 'How do I find
My gold; tell me, where do I start?'
'Look at the rainbow, close your eyes
And wish for it with all your heart.'

So Jolie did just that and knew
Just what sort of wish she would make.
The kind of gold she'd like to find
Was a huge slice of chocolate cake!

Then Jim Jew closed his eyes as well
And thought hard about his toadstool.
He wished there could be more than one,
Now that would be really cool!

So they all stood under the trees,
Sheltering from the heavy rain
Until the rainbow disappeared
And dark clouds took over again.

'I'd best take Smokey Ash inside,'
Said Jolie 'Before he gets cold.
Mummy said not to stay out long;
I'd better do as I've been told.'

So she said goodbye to her friends
And then ran back inside the house.
It had been a rather dull day
For Jolie and her little mouse.

But Mummy had a nice surprise,
She'd made Jolie a special treat.
All afternoon she'd been baking,
And there was chocolate cake to eat!

Jim Jew left the leprechauns,
Sprinting back to his weedy home.
He could move quite fast in the rain
For a rather tubby old gnome.

When he got back he was surprised
And couldn't believe what he saw.
Instead of his single toadstool
There seemed to be one or two more!

Several more toadstools had sprouted,
Growing each second up higher.
Thank heaven for rainbows! thought Jim,
Now I've more toadstools to admire!

The Christmas Fairy

One hot summer's day in July,
Jolie sat by the shade of the trees.
It really was too warm to play
And here there was a nice cool breeze.

Out of nowhere came a fairy.
Jolie shrieked, 'My gracious goodness!'
She was covered in icicles
All dangling down from her dress!

'Why are you so cold,' asked Jolie,
'On a boiling day like today?'
'Why, this is how I always am –
Don't worry, I'm really OK!'

'You seem familiar,' mused Jolie.
'How do I know you? Let me see…
I know! You appear at Christmas,
Standing on the top of our tree!'

'Yes, you're right, I come at Christmas,
But where do you think that I go?
For the rest of the year, I mean,
When you take down the mistletoe.

'I don't just go to sleep, you know,
For fifty-odd weeks of the year.
My time is spent making patterns,
I have a glittering career!'

'I'm a snowflake designer by trade –
An important job, not a game.
I design them in such detail,
And you'll never get two the same.

'When snow clouds gather in winter,
I am always there in their midst.
With great care I craft my snowflakes
And release them, flicking my wrist.

'They float gently down from their clouds
And my heart does fair burst with pride.
Is anything more beautiful
Than a snow-filled sky, far and wide?'

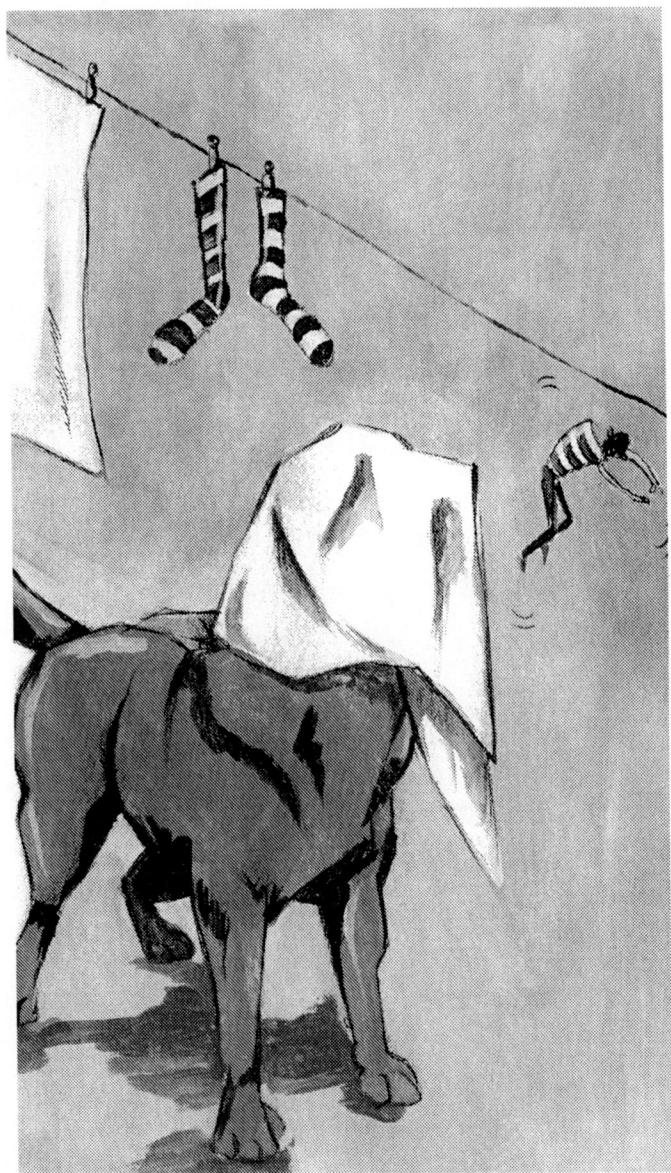

The Garden Race

Jolie's pet cat was called Tinker,
And he loved the garden so...
He spent nearly all his time there,
And all the fairies he did know.

He carried them round the garden,
Upon his strong and furry back.
He was often joined by the dog –
A Labrador, whose name was Jack.

Jolie wanted a race one day,
From the pond to the cherry tree,
The fairies would ride on Tinker
And all the elves on Jack would be.

They thought this was a great idea
And climbed up on the cat and dog.
Jolie called 'Ready, steady, *go*!'
And they set off at a fast jog.

Tinker was soon well in the lead,
Going as fast as his legs could.
The fairies clung to him tightly,
Wowee! This was ever so good!

Jack, meanwhile, was rather careless;
He ran into the washing line.
The clothes were pulled from off their pegs
And around Jack they did entwine.

Tangled up in a big white sheet,
His direction he couldn't see.
The elves jumped quickly off his back,
For they knew it was time to flee!

All elves except Lightfoot, that was,
Who still clung to Jack really tight;
But then Jack halted by the pond
And Lightfoot suddenly took flight!

He catapulted through the air
And crash-landed on a lily
The frogs just stared in shock at him.
He did feel rather silly!

Jolie quickly rescued Lightfoot,
But was worried about poor Jack.
For what would Mummy say to him?
Her white sheet was now nearly black!

Tinker then ran towards the pond
With the fairies still on his back.
They giggled helplessly, of course,
At the sight of the sheet round Jack.

Together, the fairies and elves
Managed to free Jack from the sheet.
It was rather muddy before –
Now it was trampled by their feet!

Daddy came out to the garden
And was dismayed… this wasn't good!
All the washing was on the grass
With the sheet all covered in mud.

'Now, what have you done?' gasped Daddy.
'This horrid mess, it's all too much!'
'I'll pick up the clothes,' said Jolie.
'Daddy, you don't have to touch!'

'Let's clear up this mess!' said Daddy.
'Mummy soon gets back from the shops…
I do declare,' he frowned, 'it seems
The mischief here just never stops!'

Daddy then washed the sheet again,
Jolie helped peg it on the line.
'The sun's out now,' stated Jolie,
'It'll dry soon; it will be fine.'

Daddy knew Jolie was trying
To help to put the matter right.
The fairies and elves were hiding –
It was better to keep from sight!

So Jolie had a busy day
With all the fairies and the elves.
She was so tired at bedtime
As were her little friends themselves.

That night they all slept most soundly
And were dreaming of cats and dogs.
But Lightfoot dreamed of other things,
Such as ponds and lilies and frogs!

And Jolie had a special dream,
Something so wonderful she saw.
Beside her bed was a fairy,
Much bigger than she'd seen before.

She was as tall as the ceiling,
Her wings were very different, too;
They were made just out of feathers –
Golden, and some the palest blue.

Her dress was of sparkling silver,
It seemed to shine ever so bright.
And the fairy was surrounded
By a shimmering golden light.

The fairy smiled at Jolie,
But never did utter a word.
Yet Jolie was quite certain
That beautiful music she heard.

Next day she told all the fairies
Of her strange dream the night before.
'That's not a fairy,' said Shola,
'It was an angel that you saw.'

'Oh, how wonderful!' beamed Jolie.
'Do angels tend gardens as well?'
'They look after so many things,'
Explained Shola. 'As I hear tell.'

'They care for people, too,' she said.
'There are lots of angels, you see.
They watch over and protect you;
Help you to be safe and happy.'

When Jolie went to bed that night
She thanked the angel in her prayer.
'Thank you for looking after me;
I know you will always be there.'

Angel Prayer

Whenever I doubt, whenever I fear,
I know it is then that the angels appear.
Their wings enfold me in a loving embrace,
Surrounding me always with love and with grace.

Farewell

We have come to the end of the story, or so I thought – until last night, when in my dreams I was visited by a magnificent elf. His clothes were a beautiful crimson. Although he was quite shy, he had the most endearing, mischievous grin I have ever seen! His emerald-green eyes shone with a light that danced and sparkled, the like of which I have never seen before. This is what he came to say!

'Softly
We'll tiptoe through the house,
We've got to be so quiet –
As quiet as a mouse.

'If your family hear us
All my plans will be foiled.
The party I have planned
Will truly then be spoiled.

'All my friends are waiting,
It's you they wish to see
At the bottom of the garden –
Where else would fairies be?

'They're in among the trees,
Basking in the light of the moon,
Itching to sing and dance for you
And to play you a merry tune.

'I know you believe in fairies,
I've seen those poems you write.
I think it is time you met some –
I think this very night!

'There's nothing like a fairy dance
To lighten up the heart.
And the treat we've got to eat
Is ice cream with bilberry tart.

'So come on, let's delay no more,
The fairies are waiting with glee.
This will be a fun-filled night
For you, my friend, and me.

'You can put it all in a poem –
You'll know every word to be true.
I wonder who will believe it,
Perhaps just the fairies and you!'

Lightning Source UK Ltd.
Milton Keynes UK
05 March 2010
150964UK00001B/25/A